The Official PAC Exam Guide

Professional Aptitude Council

Official Exam Guide

Professional Aptitude Council

PAC Review: The PAC Examination: Fundamentals

ISBN 978-1-60332-054-2

Copyright© 2008 Equity Press all rights reserved. No part of this publication may be reproduced, stored in a retrieval system, or transmitted in any form or by any means (electronic, mechanical, photocopying, recording or otherwise) without either the prior written permission of the publisher or a license permitting restricted copying in the United States or abroad.

The scanning, uploading and distribution of this book via the internet or via any other means without the permission of the publisher is illegal and punishable by law. Please purchase only authorized electronic editions, and do not participate in or encourage piracy of copyrighted materials.

Trademarks: All trademarks are the property of their respective owners. Neither Equity Press nor PAC is associated with any product or vender mentioned in this book.

Printed in the United States of America

The Official PAC Exam Guide

Table of Contents

Chapter 1: What is the PAC Examination: Fundamentals? 5
    What is the Professional Aptitude Council (PAC)? 6
    What is the PAC Examination? 6
    Why take the PAC Examination? 6
    What is on the PAC Examination? 7
    Examination Sections: 8
    Examination Framework 8
    Where can I take the PAC Examination? 9
    How are scores calculated? 9
    What do I do once I have my PAC Examination Score? 9
    How Can I Prepare for the PAC Examination? 10

Chapter 2: Reading Comprehension 11
    Reading Comprehension 12
    Literal Comprehension 12
    Making Inferences 13
    Quick Tips for Reading Comprehension 13
    Sharpening Your Reading Skills 14
    Tips for Using the Following Practice Sections 15
    Practice Questions 16

Chapter 3: Math Reasoning 22
    Quick Tips for Math Reasoning 23
    Mastering Math Reasoning 24
    Practice Questions 25

Chapter 4: Sentence Structure 30
    Quick Tips for Sentence Structure 31
    Developing stronger writing skills 32
    Sample Questions 33
    Practice Questions 34

Chapter 5: Logic Diagramming 38
Quick Tips Logic Diagramming 39
Understanding Workflows 39
Sample Questions 40
Practice Questions 43

Chapter 6: IT Reasoning 47
Data Sufficiency Questions 48
Logic Symbolizing Questions 49
Logic Ordering 49
Quick Tips 49
Sharpening Your Logic Skills 50
Practice Questions 51

Chapter 7: Attention to detail 58
Quick Tips for Attention to Detail 59
Developing an Eye for Detail 59
Practice Questions 60

Chapter 1: What is the PAC Examination: Fundamentals?

What is the Professional Aptitude Council (PAC)?

Based in Palo Alto, CA with offices in Bangalore, India and Shanghai, China, the Professional Aptitude Council (PAC) strives to connect you to some of the world's leading global technological corporations. We are a diverse group of individuals working to give you access to the resources you need in order to build a career that you love.

What is the PAC Examination?

Featuring both aptitude and technical assessments, PAC creates and administers a number of PAC Examinations. This guide features the PAC Examination: Fundamentals, geared towards gauging the aptitude of computer and software engineers with 0-3 years of experience. It is a 40-minute assessment composed of 45 questions designed to give you a platform on which you can display your skills to potential employers.

Rather than measuring your level of expertise in a particular area of study, the PAC Examination tests your aptitude in the areas of math, logic and English. The aim of the assessment is to give you access to numerous exciting employment opportunities by allowing you to show employers that you have the skills necessary to succeed no matter where you're from.

Why take the PAC Examination?

The PAC Examination is your key to accessing employment opportunities with some of the top technical companies in the world. As PAC has exclusive relationships with leading global technology firms, the PAC Examination is the first step to beginning a career at a world-class company. Once you've taken the PAC Examination, you will have more than just a score, you will have access to a multitude of exciting job opportunities.

Because the PAC Examination tests an individual's aptitude, rather than expertise, success on the exam means opportunities for positions that may currently be above and beyond your reach. Thousands of students just like you are now working at first-rate companies because employers saw their PAC Examination results.

What is on the PAC Examination?

There are a total of six sections on the PAC Examination evaluating your skills in the areas of math, logic and the English language: Math Reasoning, Sentence Structure, IT Reasoning, Reading Comprehension, Logic Diagramming and Attention to Detail.

The question types that appear in this guide will all be on the PAC Examination; however, they will appear in a different format:

- One question at a time will appear on the computer screen with the question and related content appearing on the top half of the page, while the answer options will appear on the bottom half of the page.
- You will select your answer using the computer. Each answer will have a circle to the left of it. In order to select an answer, you will click on the circle for the answer you have chosen, then click the answer button.
- You cannot leave an answer blank. You must mark an answer to move on to the next question. You will also NOT be able to return to a question in order to make changes.

Below is an image of what the screen will look like.

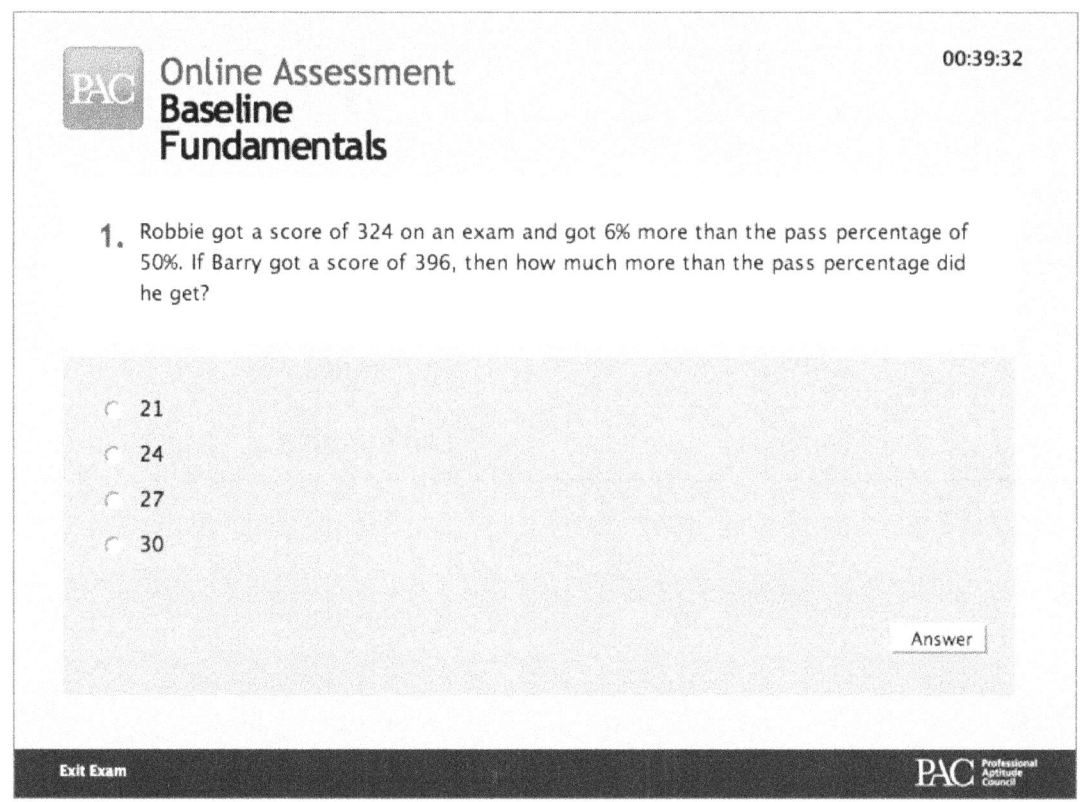

Fig. 1 – PAC assessment screen

Professional Aptitude Council

To learn more about the sections on the PAC Examination, check out the later chapters in order to better understand the skills each section tests for as well as get tips on acing each section.

Examination Sections:
Math Reasoning
Sentence Structure
IT Reasoning
Reading Comprehension
Logic Diagramming
Attention to Detail

Examination Framework

Section	# of Problems	# of Questions	Time Limit
Math Reasoning		10	10 minutes
Sentence Structure		10	7 minutes
IT Reasoning		5	6 minutes
Reading Comprehension	1	5	7 minutes
Logic Diagramming	1	5	8 minutes
Attention to Detail	1	10	2 minutes
Total		45	40 minutes

The Official PAC Exam Guide

Where can I take the PAC Examination?

The PAC Examination is an online assessment available by invitation only during secure testing windows designated by PAC. In order to learn more about taking the examination, go to www.pacexam.com and create an online account with PAC.

How are scores calculated?

Scores are calculated based on the number of questions you answer correctly out of the total number of questions. Each question is worth one point. If you do not complete the assessment within the time limit, any question that you have not answered will be counted as incorrect. You will be placed within a bracket based on how well you performed in relation to your peers, and potential employers will be able to compare scores.

Your PAC Examination score is valid for five years and can be presented to potential employers who use it as part of their screening process. If you are not happy with your score, you can retake the PAC Examination once every three months.

What do I do once I have my PAC Examination Score?

Getting a PAC Examination score is just the beginning! Once you have taken a PAC Examination, potential employers will have the capacity to view your score and offer you job opportunities. While employers will have access to your scores, you have to make sure you get noticed, and PAC is committed to helping you stand out with Propel. A unique global medium for job seekers to attract company attention, Propel empowers candidates to comprehensively highlight their technical, intellectual and professional excellence beyond the typical resume. Generate interest in your skills by creating your Propel profile at www.pacexam.com.

How is the PAC Examination developed?

A diverse panel of individuals are responsible for the content of the PAC Examination. These individuals regularly write, review and revise the wide variety of questions that ultimately appear on the exam. Questions are tested and reviewed thoroughly before they are presented to you in the PAC Examination. In addition, questions are continually reviewed for their efficacy in fairly measuring candidate skills.

How Can I Prepare for the PAC Examination?

Below are test taking tips to use the day of the PAC Examination. Check out the following chapters in order to learn specifics excelling on the PAC Examination.

Test Taking Tips

- Be sure to have paper and pencils with you when you are taking the PAC Examination. As you are not able to write on the computer screen, you must use scratch paper in order to work out your answers.
- Before you begin the exam online, make sure that you have at least 40 minutes when you will be uninterrupted in order to complete the exam.
- If possible, when you access the PAC Examination online, choose a location that has the most reliable internet connection and power source available to you. This will decrease the chances of encountering technical errors during the course of your test.
- If taking the exam in a noisy atmosphere, such as an internet café, consider bringing ear plugs with you in order to block out the noise while you are taking the exam.

Chapter 2: Reading Comprehension

Reading Comprehension

The reading comprehension section measures your ability to understand the English language in its written form. Not only are you expected to be able to read and understand a passage, you will also be tested on your ability to draw conclusions from both the literal and implied meanings present in the written sample. These types of questions help employers understand the degree to which you would be able to understand directions, business communications, and even just simple exchanges via inter-office email. Even though the PAC Examination is designed for individuals who plan to enter professions in the IT industry, strong communication skills are still needed in order to be a successful computer programmer or engineer. Most likely you will be working with a wide range of individuals with whom you will need to communicate ideas, goals, expectations, strategies and deadlines on a wide range of projects; therefore, you must have effective communication skills.

The reading comprehension section has five questions that you will have seven minutes to answer. Each section begins with a 300-350 word passage on a general topic. You do not need to have prior knowledge of the topic as the questions are focused on your ability to comprehend the passage, rather than apply previous knowledge. On the instructions page, you will be presented with the reading comprehension passage. The passage will also be present on each of the pages of the questions that you need to answer in this section.

The questions may ask for specific information that is in the passage, or the questions may ask you to make an inference based on the information that is presented in the passage.

Literal Comprehension

Once you have read a passage, a question may ask for a specific fact or piece of information. For example, in a general reading passage about elephants that describes their habits, characteristics and where they are found in the wild, a question might ask you to list in what countries elephants are present, as well as basic descriptions of their habits and lives. These questions ask you to understand the information you have just read and apply it to what is being asked.

Although the passages will not be that complex, it is very difficult to study for this section as you cannot predict what topic or vocabulary will be presented within the passage. The Quick Tips section covers test-taking strategies to help you with this part of the test as well as what to do in the event that you encounter words with which you are not familiar.

Making Inferences

While some questions will ask you to present information directly stated in the passage, other questions will ask you to draw conclusions based on what you have just read. In these questions, there will not be a direct answer presented to you in the passage, but rather you will have to use your reasoning abilities in order to choose the answer that logically makes sense given the context and information presented in the passage.

Even though this may sound intimidating, remember that the information needed to answer the question is still within the passage, you just have to connect that information in the most reasonable manner in order to answer these questions.

Quick Tips for Reading Comprehension

Here are key steps to use when you're answering reading comprehension questions:

1. First, initially skim the passage. In this first reading, don't worry about the details. Merely try to figure out what the passage is about.
2. When given a question about the passage, read the question and ignore the answer choices. Then, look for key words in the question within the context of the passage. This is particularly helpful if you are stumped as to the meaning of a word, or you have been presented with vocabulary with which you are unfamiliar.
3. If you can't figure out the answer to the question, then look at your answer options and do your best to figure out which is the best match.
4. When you encounter a word that is unfamiliar to you, and you are asked to define it, look at the context of it in order to come up with a reasonable definition. Based on the definition you come up with, choose the best answer from the options presented.
5. Don't focus on memorizing details in the passage as you can always look back at the passage if a question asks for a specific piece of information.
6. Remember that the questions test you on the information given to you in the passage. If the passage is about, say, motorcycles, and if gives you information that conflicts with your own experiences, answer the questions as though the information in the passage is correct. Your own knowledge, in this case, is not what is being tested, but rather it is your ability to read and understand a piece of information that is most important here.

Sharpening Your Reading Skills

The greatest way that you can improve your reading comprehension skills is by reading more. Reading more not only strengthens your comprehension skills, but also expands your vocabulary and understanding of a variety of subjects.

Employers are impressed by students that not only have strong skills associated with technical positions, but that also have the ability to communicate with colleagues and supervisors across disciplines. When working as part of a team, it is particularly important that you are able to not only read the text and information presented to you in various formats such as email, but that you are also able to respond appropriately to the tones expressed through a particular medium of communication. The more you increase the amount you read as well as the variety of material that you read, the more sophisticated your understanding of the English language will be. As your ability to handle the English language grows, you will position yourself to be a promising candidate that brings key technical and communication skills to a corporation.

What should you read? Start right where you are. If your school or town has a local newspaper, take the time to read it. Begin reading one of the national newspapers, and pay particular attention to the business section in order to learn more about companies that interest you.

Additionally, consider reading about topics that are not necessarily related to the technology field. Browsing English-language newspapers or even reading English-language literature can prepare you to not only handle the language, but can also prepare you to identify aspects of foreign, English-speaking cultures that are perhaps unfamiliar or surprising to you. Taking advantage of the internet and reading foreign English language media may give you a clue as to idiomatic expressions and slang that you could encounter once on the job.

When you encounter unfamiliar words when reading, you may want to write them down and look up their definitions. As you do this and continue to review the material, you will gradually build your vocabulary. In addition, there are services on the web that can send you an English word a day so that you can gradually increase your English word bank. While all this information may seem daunting, remember that reading every day, even for only ten minutes, will improve the speed and accuracy with which you read English.

Tips for Using the Following Practice Sections

Although you will not be taking the following practice questions on a computer, there are other ways in which you can mimic the conditions in which you'll be taking the test. For instance, try to time yourself and see how long it takes you to answer the questions. Then compare the amount of time you took to complete the questions, compare it with the amount of time that you will be given during the exam and figure out how you can best maximize your time. Also, make sure you have no distractions and are able to focus on what you're doing.

The tips given above work well for many people; however, not everyone is the same. Try the tips given here and modify them according to your needs. Good luck!

Professional Aptitude Council

Practice Questions

Instructions (these are the instructions you will see when taking the test):

This is the reading comprehension section. It is designed to test your ability to understand the English language in written form as well as draw logical conclusions based on the information presented in the passage. This section has 1 reading passage and 5 questions pertaining the passage that you must answer. You will have 7 minutes to complete this section (NOTE: on the real examination you will only have to answer 5 questions; however, there are 10 questions below connected to the following passage).

Below are images of what the Reading Comprehension will look like on the computer screen. Please note that during the exam after you have read the passage you will need to scroll down in order to read the question and answer options.

The Official PAC Exam Guide

 **Online Assessment**
PAC Guide question

00:00:00

1. Social Networking

   A social networking profile is an online feature that individuals can use to share information about themselves with others over the Internet. They often include the option for users to include their name, contact information, relationship status, interests, a self-statement describing themselves and a profile photo. Individuals use these online profiles to connect with people who share similar interests and even form online communities through a variety of virtual groups present on the world wide web.

   Social networking profiles are a fascinating exercise on the tangible construction of self-identity. Through a social networking profile users are able to visually and tangibly construct their identity, or rather they can articulate how they perceive themselves through their online profiles. They have control over what profile photo they put up and what information they make available for others to see. In general, people put up flattering or funny profile photos of themselves, but sometimes people use photos that do not include their own image, but that reveal something about their personality.

   In addition, the information that users do (or do not) provide within their profiles communicates a great deal about them. Information such as relationship status expresses what and who matters to a user. For example, users who explicitly state that they are in a relationship are expressing that their relationship holds great significance for them and that it may be a key part of how they define themselves. In contrast, individuals who do not include a statement that reveals their relationship status are potentially expressing that they want their personal lives to remain private and not visible to others online.

   Another way through which individuals on social networking sites construct their identities is through the groups or online communities they choose to join. Joining different groups that have a variety of themes such as celebrating a home town,

status are potentially expressing that they want their personal lives to remain private and not visible to others online.

Another way through which individuals on social networking sites construct their identities is through the groups or online communities they choose to join. Joining different groups that have a variety of themes such as celebrating a home town, family origin, interests, or inside jokes is like putting together pieces of a jigsaw puzzle. Users are able to connect idiosyncratic elements in order to reveal the way that they think about themselves. Not only do users have the opportunity to include surface information such as where they're from, through the groups they express their values, priorities, interests and quirks. In a way, social networking profiles give individuals the opportunity to put together an identity that includes the various aspects of their temperament include the serious and fun parts.

Based on the passage, which of the following BEST defines a social networking profile?

○ A digital profile that individuals use to connect with others online

○ An online profile used by job seekers to state their professional goals and qualifications

○ A venue for individuals to post digital images of themselves and their online community

○ An online medium through which users can express their personality

Social Networking

A social networking profile is an online feature that individuals can use to share information about themselves with others over the Internet. They often include the option for users to include their names, contact information, relationship statuses, interests, self-statements describing themselves as well as profile photos. Individuals use these online profiles to connect with people who share similar interests and even form online communities through a variety of virtual groups present on the world wide web.

Social networking profiles are fascinating exercises on the tangible construction of self-identity. Through a social networking profile, users are able to visually construct their identities, or rather they can articulate how they perceive themselves through their online profiles. They have control over what profile photos they put up and what information they make available for others to see. In general, people put up flattering or funny profile photos of themselves, but sometimes people use photos that do not include their own images, but that reveal something about their personalities.

In addition, the information that users do (or do not) provide within their profiles communicates a great deal about them. Information such as relationship status expresses what and who matters to a user. For example, users who explicitly state that they are in relationships are expressing that their relationships hold great significance for them and that they may be a key part of how they define themselves. In contrast, individuals who do not include a statement that reveals their relationship status are potentially expressing that they want their personal lives to remain private and not visible to others online.

Another way through which individuals on social networking sites construct their identities is through the groups or online communities they choose to join. Joining different groups that have a variety of themes such as celebrating a hometown, family origin, interests, or inside jokes is like putting together pieces of a jigsaw puzzle. Users are able to connect idiosyncratic elements in order to reveal the way that they think about themselves. Not only do users have the opportunity to include surface information such as where they're from, through the groups they express their values, priorities, interests and quirks.

1. Based on the passage, which of the following BEST defines a social networking profile?

    A. A digital profile that individuals use to connect with others online

    B. An online profile used by job seekers to state their professional goals and qualifications

    C. A venue for individuals to post digital images of themselves and their online communities

    D. An online medium through which users can express their personalities

2. What does the author mean when he/she says: "Social networking profiles are a fascinating exercise on the tangible construction of self-identity."

   A. Social networking profiles are a unique medium through which individuals explicitly share with others how they see themselves

   B. Social networking profiles allow individuals to see how others perceive them

   C. Social networking profiles are a medium through which users can engage in self reflection

   D. Social networking profiles are a unique way for individuals to hone their social skills.

3. According to the passage, what are the most common types of profile photos that are posted on social networking profiles?

   A. Flattering self images
   B. Amusing self images
   C. Images that reveal something about a user's personality
   D. All of the above

4. Based on the passage, what are individuals who include their relationship status on their social networking profiles expressing?

   A. They are stating that they do not want individuals online to contact them concerning starting a romantic relationship
   B. They are expressing that their relationships with their partners are key parts of who they are
   C. They are trying to embarrass their partners by publicly stating their relationship status
   D. They are negating the importance of their relationships with their partners

5. Based on the passage, when individuals do not include their relationship statuses on their profiles, which of the following statements communicates what they want to express to others who view their profiles?

   A. "Whether I'm in a relationship or not doesn't matter to me."
   B. "I'm ashamed that I'm not in a relationship, so I'd rather not make it public."
   C. "I prefer to keep my personal life private."
   D. "I don't update my social networking profile often."

6. Based on the passage, what does "idiosyncratic" mean?

A. A feature that is unusual or particularly distinguishing in nature
B. A feature that is exceptionally negative, and therefore distinguishing in nature
C. A feature that is particularly positively, and therefore distinguishing in nature
D. A feature that is disconnected from a person's general personality, and therefore distinguishing in nature

7. Which word best describes the tone of the passage?

    A. Excited
    B. Analytical
    C. Persuasive
    D. Reflective

8. This article would most likely appear in:

    A. A science and technology journal
    B. A newspaper's editorial section
    C. A popular technology magazine
    D. An individual's personal blog

9. Based on the passage, what are other ways that individuals might use social networking profiles that are not listed here?

    A. Connecting with others concerning potential job opportunities
    B. Reuniting with childhood friends
    C. Selling and buying used items to individuals online
    D. All of the above

10. Which of the following lists best describe the common elements that make up a social networking profile?

    A. Contact information and relationship status
    B. Self-statement, relationship status and profile photo
    C. Contact information and profile photo
    D. Contact information, self-statement, profile photo, interests and relationship status

Chapter 3: Math Reasoning

The Official PAC Exam Guide

Math Reasoning

The math reasoning section tests your ability to understand and implement mathematical principles within concrete circumstances. While you probably won't be asked to sit down and solve these kinds of questions in a work environment, these questions help employers see how well you understand and apply mathematical principles to real world situations.

When working as a software or computer engineer, you will need to use particular mathematical concepts in order to solve a variety of challenges that will arise as you develop processes or implement systems. Potential employers need to know if you understand what principles to use in a given situation as well as if you are able to effectively employ those principles in order to solve the problem. Being comfortable with math can also indicate comfort with logic and basic reasoning. It also can tell your potential employer how well you cope with numbers in general.

Quick Tips for Math Reasoning

Here are four steps to use when you're solving a math reasoning problem:

1. Understand the problem. Identify the specific quantity you need to find and the problem that the question is asking you to solve.
2. Make a plan. Think about the techniques that would work best to solve the problem.
3. Put your plan into action.
4. Evaluate. In light of the question's context, review whether your answer is reasonable. Be sure to also take note of the techniques that worked in solving this question, so that you can apply them to similar problems in the future.
5. If you are feeling uncomfortable with the problem, you can plug numbers from your answer choices into the question and see which one works. Start with the middle number. The result should tell you if you need to select higher numbers to plug in, or lower numbers.

Mastering Math Reasoning

While math reasoning problems can seem daunting because of all of the information presented in them, math reasoning problems are just mathematical problems expressed in words, within the context of a specific situation. All you have to do is reorganize the information so that you can see and solve the mathematical problem.

After reading a problem, draw an image that depicts the scenario. Include and label the quantities in the question. For quantities that are not a fixed number, use a variable (eg the letter x or y) to represent them. Next, understand the goal of the problem and figure out what equations best reflect how the different variables relate to each other; express the goal of the problem in mathematical terms.

Solve the mathematical representation of the problem using the best techniques.

Once you've solved the problem mathematically, put it back into words, so that you can see how the answer relates to the original problem.

Taken and revised from "Success in Mathematics," the Saint Louis University Department of Mathematics and Computer Science, http://euler.slu.edu/Dept/SuccessinMath.html, June 1993.

The principles expressed are from, George Pólya's, How to Solve It, Princeton University Press, Princeton (1945).

Practice Questions

Instructions (these are the instructions you will see when taking the test):

This is the Math Reasoning section. It is designed to test your ability to understand and implement mathematical principles within concrete circumstances. You will have 11 minutes to complete the 10 questions in this section.

1. Jonas collects x signatures per hour on his petition and works y hours in month one. In month two, he collects 10% more signatures per hour, but works 10% fewer hours. How many signatures did he collect in the second month compared to the first?
A. the same
B. fewer
C. more
D. exactly one fewer than last month

2. A corporation increases its revenues by 10% each month from the prior month. If we begin in January, in what month would our revenues first surpass twice the amount that they were in January?
A. August
B. September
C. October
D. November

3. Donna completes x reports in an hour and Denise completes y reports in an hour. How many reports are produced when Denise works H hours and Donna works L hours more than Denise?
A. L(x+y)-x
B. H(y+x+L)
C. yH+x(H+L)
D. (x+y)H+yL

4. If Sumeet earns twice as much hourly as Amit, and Sumeet works two and a half times as many hours in a month as Amit, what is the ratio of Sumeet's monthly earnings to those of Amit?
A. 2.5:1
B. 2:1
C. 4.5:1
D. 5:1

Professional Aptitude Council

5. Process A runs in 30 seconds on one processor and process B runs in 40 seconds on that same processor. If the two are set to run simultaneously on a two processor machine and process A runs half as fast and process B only sees a 10% increase in run time, how long does it take to complete both processes on the two processor machine?

A. 44 seconds
B. 74 seconds
C. 60 seconds
D. 104 seconds

6. Colin is diligent about his savings plan. From his regular job, he earns J dollars a week, of which he saves x percent. In addition, he has a small business that he runs at night. From this business where he earns K dollars a week, he saves 40% of the first L dollars he earns and 75% of anything he earns above that. You may assume the K is larger than L. How much does Colin save each week?

A. xJ+ 0.4 +0.75L
B. x(J + 0.4K + 0.75L)
C. xJ + 0.4K +0.75(L-K)
D. xJ + 0.4L + 0.75(K-L)

7. A car has a 22-gallon gas tank and gets 24 miles to the gallon. You must fill your tank before it's totally empty, so assume you can use 20 gallons before you refill. If you assume you start with a full tank and need to complete a 1200-mile trip, how many times do you need to refill?
A. 4
B. 3
C. 2
D. 5

8. Which of the following most closely represents a 22% failure rate?
A. 4 out of 16 fail
B. 6 out of 27 fail
C. 16 out of 64 fail
D. 4 out of 14 fail

9. If an empty jug weighs x pounds and can hold y pounds of water, how much does the Jug weigh when it's z % empty?

A. x + yz
B. x + y - z
C. x + (1-z)y
D. x + (1-yz)

10. Darts are thrown at a dart board and each dart scores as follows: a dart that lands in a number between one and twenty can also land in a double score" or "triple score" such that the most one dart can score is 60 points ("triple score 20"). To win the game, the player must accumulate exactly 177 points and throw at least one "double score." What is the fewest number of darts with which the game can be won?

A. 3
B. 4
C. 5
D. 6

11. A building is 8 meters by 11 meters and 4 meters tall. The outside will be covered with panels that are 2 meters by 1 meter. Panels may not be cut and used in parts. What is the fewest number of panels required to cover the entire outside of the building?

A. 38
B. 42
C. 76
D. 80

12. A sales force sells 250 units a month and all sales people sell identical amounts. If the size of the sales force is increased by 10%, but sales per salesperson is 10% less, what will happen to sales?

A. stay the same
B. increase
C. decrease
D. not enough information to know

13. If a production line has a 9% defect rate and produces 770 units a day, how many products will be defective?

A. 63
B. 70
C. 69
D. 72

14. A jar can hold exactly 510 coins and weighs 21 grams when empty. Each coin weighs exactly one gram. How much does the jar weigh when it's one third full?

A. 201.0 grams
B. 180.1 grams
C. 184.3 grams
D. 191.0 grams

15. Tommy is a 10-year-old boy. In each of the next 4 years his weight will increase by 10%. By what percentage in total will his weight increase from his present weight?
A. 40%
B. 44%
C. 46%
D. 47%

16. An airline assumes that on average each passenger weighs x pounds. It also assumes that 80% of passengers will have luggage that on average weighs y pounds. In addition to passengers, each airplane carries freight and the airline assumes that each container weighs z pounds. How would you calculate the expected weight of a plane scheduled to carry P passengers and F freight containers?

A. 0.8Px + Py + Fz
B. 0.8(Px + Py) + Fz
C. P(x + .8y)Fz
D. P(x + .8y) + Fz

17. A rug merchant sells rugs in three sizes. The small rugs sell for 500 Euros, the medium rugs for 600 Euros and the large rugs sell for 900 Euros. Which of the scenarios below will produce the most income for the merchant?

A. sell 10 small and 4 medium rugs
B. sell 6 small, 4 medium and 2 large rugs
C. sell 8 large rugs
D. sell 12 small and 2 medium rugs

18. If it takes a program .01 second to read a piece of data from memory and .1 second to read the same piece of data from disk, how long would it take to read 26,000 pieces of such data if 20% of it could be loaded into memory in advance, and the rest had to be read from disk?

A. 2366 seconds
B. 260 seconds
C. 2132 seconds
D. 236.6 seconds

19. Amit borrows RMB 20,000 from the bank to purchase a new car. The bank agrees to lend the money at a simple interest annual rate of 8%. How much does Amit need to give the bank to repay the loan in 1 year and 6 months?

A. 2,400
B. 16,000
C. 24,000
D. 22,400
E. 44,200

20. Lee falls in a 50-foot hole. Each day, Lee can climb up 3 feet. But Lee must also rest each day and that causes him to slide back down the hole 2 feet per day. Assuming Lee starts climbing at the beginning of a day, what is the minimum number of days he needs to climb out of the hole? (Select the best possible answer from the options below.)
A. 51 days
B. 50 days
C. 49 days
D. 48 days
E. None of the Above

Chapter 4: Sentence Structure

Sentence Structure

The sentence structure section tests for two areas: 1) your ability to form logical ideas and effectively organize the different parts of a sentence using the English language and 2) the scope of your vocabulary and your ability to understand and use it within a specific context.

Just as with reading comprehension questions, it is important to show employers that you have excellent communication skills in addition to your technical skills. The possession of both types of skills will enable you to effectively work on a team in order to design and implement the systems needed by potential employers. After all, you will not only need to understand directions, but possibly give them as well. You will need to compose memos and emails and potentially give presentations. Of the four language skills of talking, listening, reading, and writing, this test assesses your ability to read and write.

The sentence structure section has 10 questions that you will have 7 minutes to complete. In order to answer the questions, you will need to complete a sentence by choosing the most appropriate answer option available. The questions will require you to either choose the answer option that forms the most logical idea or the word that best completes the sentence. Questions of the former type are called "Causation" questions, and those questions of the latter type are called "Vocabulary" questions. Examples of these questions can be found in the "Practice Questions" section.

Quick Tips for Sentence Structure

Here are key steps to use when you're answering sentence structure questions (view the practice questions for examples of each):

1. Look at key words to help you identify the relationships between the parts of the sentence that need to be completed.

2. When trying to identify the best word to complete a sentence, consider the connotation, or contextual meaning of a word.
3. Being able to identify the grammatical function of a word is also helpful.
    a.   For instance, in English, the ending "-er" often indicates a comparative relationship. For example: this one is bett**er** than that one.
    b.   The suffix –ly is often indicative of an adverb. For example, "she worked quick**ly**."
    c.   The suffix "-ed" often indicates a past participle or the presence of a compound verb. For example, "the woman is divorc**ed**" or "the computer has work**ed**"
    d.   You can also use your understanding of words you already know to make inferences about new words. Although the English language does not have a root system as some other languages do, there are some consistencies in word origin, or etymology, that you may want to memorize. For instance, the term "bio" generally has to do with the word "life." Similarly, the term "libro" often corresponds with ideas or concepts connected to books or places of learning. As you must provide an answer for every question on the PAC Examination, having a working

knowledge of prefixes, suffixes, or etymologies can help you make good guesses in the instances where you are unsure of an answer.
4. Using your knowledge of prefixes and suffixes such as those above can help you even if you don't know some of the words in the list of answer choices.

Developing stronger writing skills

While you are not actively writing in sentence structure questions, they are testing for your ability to not only understand, but form logical ideas. In other words, they are seeing how well you communicate in written form. Sometimes students interested in careers in technology neglect the opportunity to develop their writing skills thinking that as a computer programmer they won't need to know how to write well. Even though you will not use writing in the same capacity as other professions, the ability to write clearly and logically is vitally important within technology professions.

What are some things you can do to improve your writing skills? It might seem strange, but read more. Reading more exposes you to a variety of writing styles and helps you to better identify the elements that make for strong writing. When reading English language texts, try to read actively. That is, if you don't understand why a word was used in a particular context, look it up in a dictionary or grammatical reference. Keep an eye out for uses of the language that don't seem to be consistent with grammatical rules and make sure that you understand the reason for the inconsistency as well as how it can be corrected.

Another key way to develop your writing abilities is to write more. After reading articles or books, take the opportunity to write out your opinions, thoughts and questions on the subject. Once you've put down your thoughts, consider if the ideas you expressed are presented in a logic order, if you've chosen precise language to explain your perspective and if the structure of the sentences makes sense. You can even have a friend, parent or teacher look over your work and give you feedback. You can also use the internet to develop your writing skills by commenting on English language blogs or newspapers. Once you've read a piece in a newspaper, consider writing a letter to the editor, if it was on a website or blog, a message to the author. The better you are able to organize and express your thoughts in written form, the better you will be able to communicate important technical principles and ideas when in a work environment.

Sample Questions

Instructions (these are the instructions you will see when taking the test)::

This is the Sentence Structure section. It is designed to test your ability to form logical ideas and effectively organize the different parts of a sentence. You will have 7 minutes to complete the 10 questions in this section.

1. **"Although he bought a _____ bicycle, the tires _____ quickly."**

    a. old...wore out
    b. new...worked
    c. previously owned...broke
    d. new...wore out (CORRECT)

The word "although" signals that the two parts of the sentence have a contrasting relationship; therefore, a particular outcome would be expected from the first part of the sentence ("Although he bought _____ bicycle,"), yet the opposite of the expected outcome occurred in the second half of the sentence ("the tires _____ quickly.").

Based on this information, it makes the most sense to choose answer option 'd' (new...wore out) because while you would expect that the tires on a new bicycle would last a long time, the tires actually wore out sooner than expected.

2. **"Peter's data was _____; therefore, we weren't able to reach a conclusion."**

    a. destitute
    b. deficient (CORRECT)
    c. rudimentary
    d. profuse

The second half of the sentence communicates that there was some characteristic about the data that prevented a conclusion from being drawn, so you can expect that the appropriate word to complete the sentence should express a sense of lacking.

Answer option 'd', "profuse" can be eliminated immediately as it portrays a sense of abundance. The other three answer options all seem to convey a sense of being incomplete; however, consider the intensity of the word as well as the context in which it is generally used. Answer option 'a', "destitute," is generally used to describe an intense situation, and answer option 'c', "rudimentary," does not have enough intensity. Based on this information, answer option 'b', "deficient," is the best answer.

Professional Aptitude Council

Practice Questions

Causation

1. ... warmed to the proposal ... eager optimism.

A. Their supervisor ... but cautioned against
B. Their desires ... and fueled the
C. Numerous clients were ... and displayed
D. The combustible fire ... which increased our

2. The engineer is ... in the field of code writing; but his bug-fixing abilities ...
A. notorious ... are equally famous.
B. highly skilled ... are equally skilled.
C. preeminent ... are substandard.
D. excellent ... is were she needs the most improvement.

3. Neither the engineers nor the system architect ... about anything ...
A. care ... other than the client's happiness.
B. deliberate ... from the circuitous point of view.
C. cares ... other than the success of the project.
D. take accountability ... of a low priority.

4. Client feedback ranged from ..., so moving forward we will need to ...

A. superlative to astronomical ... listen more intently to the remonstrations.
B. succinct to verbose ... specify response length guidelines.
C. morose to negative ... continue the hard work and effort put forth to-date.
D. extremely positive to extra negative ... work on acting more consistent.

5. Our proposal is ... the competition as it provides ...
A. different than... for a more holistic solution.
B. different from... more features at a lower price.
C. differing from ... because we offer better value for the same price.
D. different then ... for more people to be assigned to your project.

6. The ... the new website is that it will ... the customers it was intended to attract.
A. benefit of ... repel
B. highlight of ... retract

C. attraction of ... alienate
D. issue with ... offend

7. ... for the client review, the project was ...
A. Because of ... a major success.
B. Accept ... drawing to a close.
C. Waiting ... ahead of schedule.
D. Except ... complete.

8. The project manager ... called the client immediately to ...
A. should of ... except the proposal.
B. should have ... contest their claim.
C. Were to have ... staked our our position.
D. should of ... be polite.

9. ... reviews of the situation ... in the right direction.
A. Quarterly ... ensured the project was headed
B. Frequent ... insured our automobile drove
C. Alot of ... keeps the situation conforming
D. Customer ... provided input to

10. He ... the accusation, ... to provide any corroborating evidence.

A. categorically denied ... but failed
B. resented ... yet desired
C. relented to ... and wanted
D. hated ... and angrily denied

Vocabulary

11. She was always very _____ , when arriving at the meetings.
A. haste
B. prompt
C. adroit
D. elate

12. Because it was _____ we decided to go home.
A. tardy
B. late
C. obscure
D. induce

13. Their wedding was a very _____ affair
A. scintillate
B. glamour
C. lavish
D. splendor

14. She was very _____ in her attitude.
A. haughty
B. appease
C. beseech
D. tarnish

15. They were _____ with fear as the hurricane approached.
A. rapture
B. prostate
C. profuse
D. prostrate

16. He was afraid the news would _____ his reputation.
A. tarnish
B. vulgar
C. sundry
D. cause

17. The holiday was an _____ for them to work late.
A. merit
B. intention
C. deserve
D. incentive

18. The police tried to _____ the wild crowds.
A. detail
B. deter
C. detach
D. erode

19. She was very _____, and tended to believe everything she heard.
A. astute
B. ponderous
C. plausible
D. naive

20. The job was very _____, so she often fell asleep.
A. difficult
B. enthralling
C. tedious
D. arduous

Chapter 5: Logic Diagramming

The Official PAC Exam Guide

Logic Diagramming

The logic diagramming section tests your ability to logically follow a workflow. A workflow is a term used to describe the internal design of an electronic or digital system. The essential component of what computer engineers do is design systems within a variety of different contexts. It is vitally important that you're able to create and follow logical processes that define the systems and programs you're developing. Logic diagramming questions will help potential employers evaluate your capacity for organizing information into logical and effective workflows.

The logic diagramming section has five questions that you will have eight minutes to answer. Each section begins with a diagram that represents a particular process. Along with the diagram, instructions describing the process that it is supposed to accomplish are included. The diagram will have a series of cells. Some of the cells will have functions in them; however, some of the cells will have only one number in them. You will be asked to identify the value that each of the numbered cells should have. This diagram will be available when you first read the instructions as well as on the pages of each of the questions that you need to answer for this section.

Quick Tips Logic Diagramming

1. Be sure that you understand the objective of the system being described in the diagram.
2. Pay attention to the values in the cells before and after those for which you need to find a value. They will provide you with context that will help you choose the best answer.

Understanding Workflows

A key component of working as an engineer is establishing processes that work efficiently and logically. Therefore, determining the unknown values of cells in logic diagramming questions is more than about filling in the empty spaces, but rather understanding the objective of a process and creating a workflow that functions according to it.

When approaching logic diagramming questions, be sure that you understand the objective of the system that is being described. Based on the objective, briefly sketch out for yourself how the workflow will function. This is not a detailed diagram, but rather a picture meant to give you a quick idea of how the various parts of the process need to fit together. Once you have done this, pay attention to the cells that come before and after the empty cells in the online diagram in order to give you the context for defining the missing elements in the workflow. Before looking at the answer options, determine what values each cell should have. Once you fill in the elements, go through the workflow and see if it makes sense. Based on your answers, choose the best answer option from those available.

When you want to look at more complex processes, search on the Internet for diagrams of electronic and computer programs. Study the diagrams in order to understand the relationship between the different elements. By engaging in these exercises, you'll gain a better understanding of how to create a logical workflow

Sample Questions

Instructions (these are the instructions you will see when taking the test):

This is the Logic Diagramming section. It is designed test your ability to follow a workflow in a logical manner. You will be presented with one diagram depicting a particular workflow to which you will refer for the following 5 questions. You will have 8 minutes to complete this section.

Below is an image of what the Logic Diagramming question will look like on the computer screen. Please note that during the exam you will need to scroll down in order to view the question and answer options below the image.

Online Assessment
Baseline Fundamentals

00:31:52

31. The next five questions are based on the following flowchart.

The following flowchart tracks the score in a game played with a box containing balls of 2 colors. One ball is drawn at a time and the score advances by 2 if a particular colored ball is preceded by an even number of balls of the same color and decreases by 1 if a particular colored ball is preceded by an odd number of balls of the same color. The minimum score during the game is zero, and the game ends when the score reaches 20.

Each ball has the attribute BCOL and the two colors are stored in the variables COL1 and COL2. The number of balls drawn of each of these colors is stored in NUM1 and NUM2.

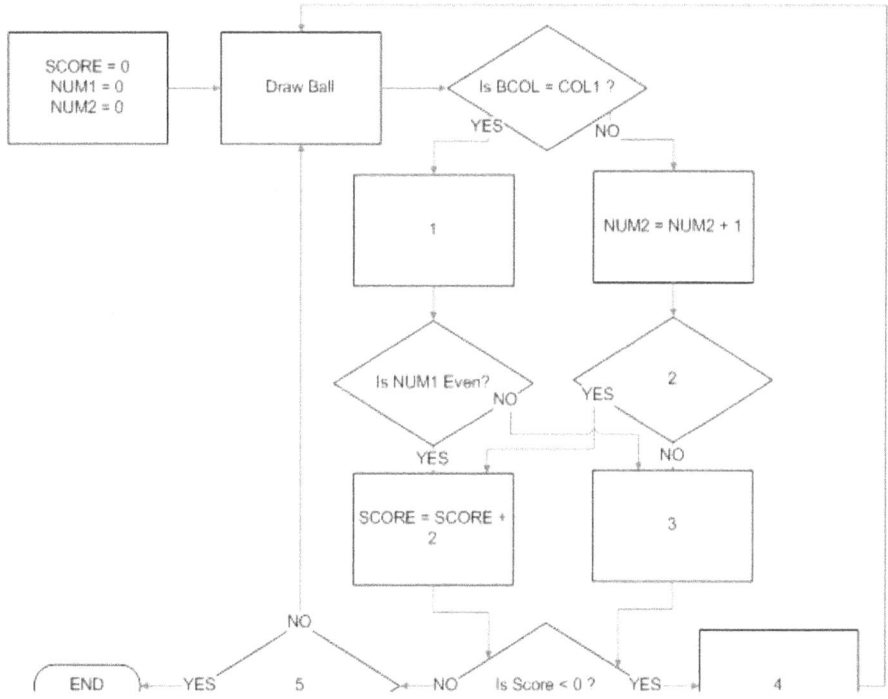

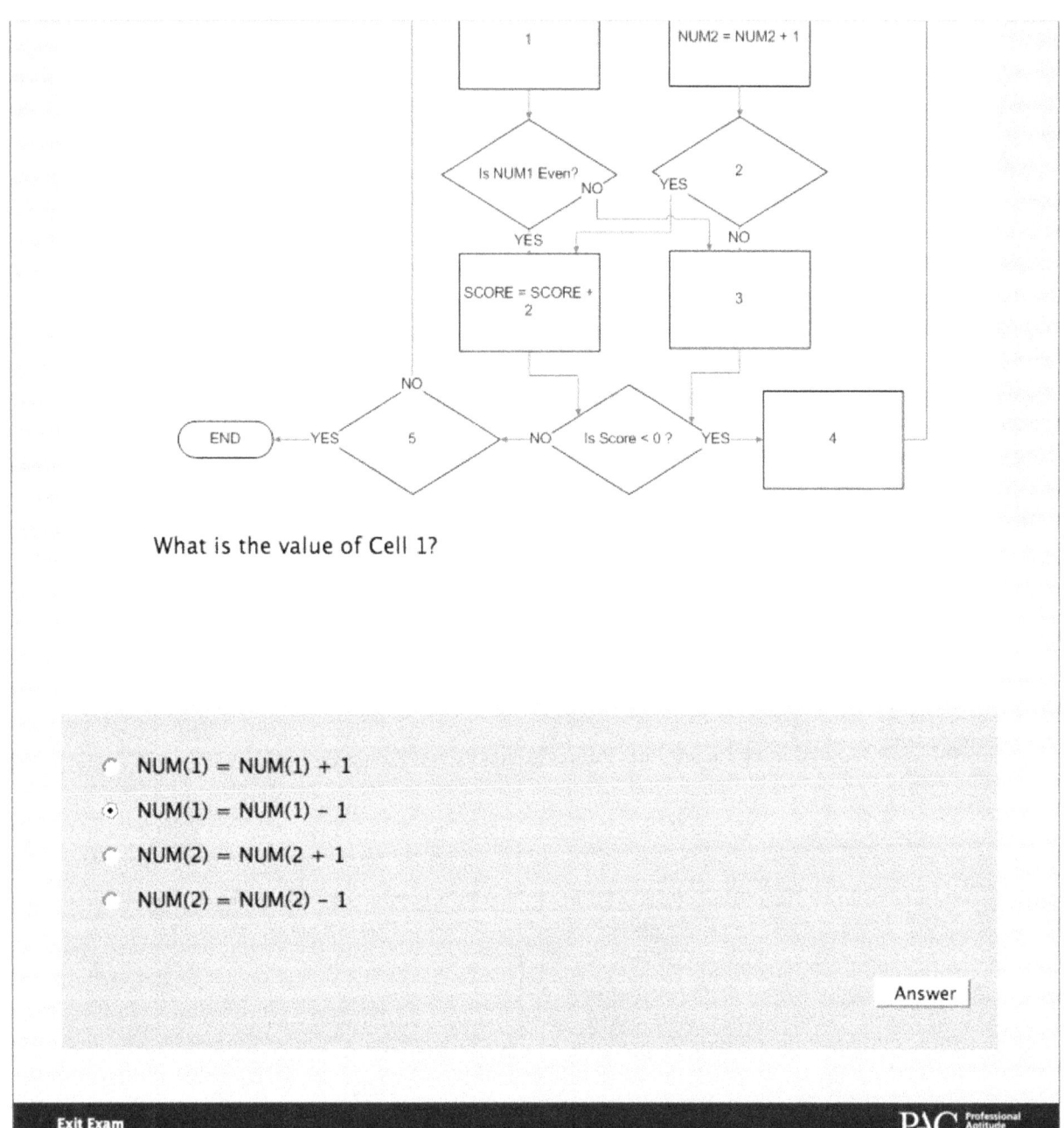

What is the value of Cell 1?

- ○ NUM(1) = NUM(1) + 1
- ◉ NUM(1) = NUM(1) - 1
- ○ NUM(2) = NUM(2 + 1
- ○ NUM(2) = NUM(2) - 1

Practice Questions

Diagram 1

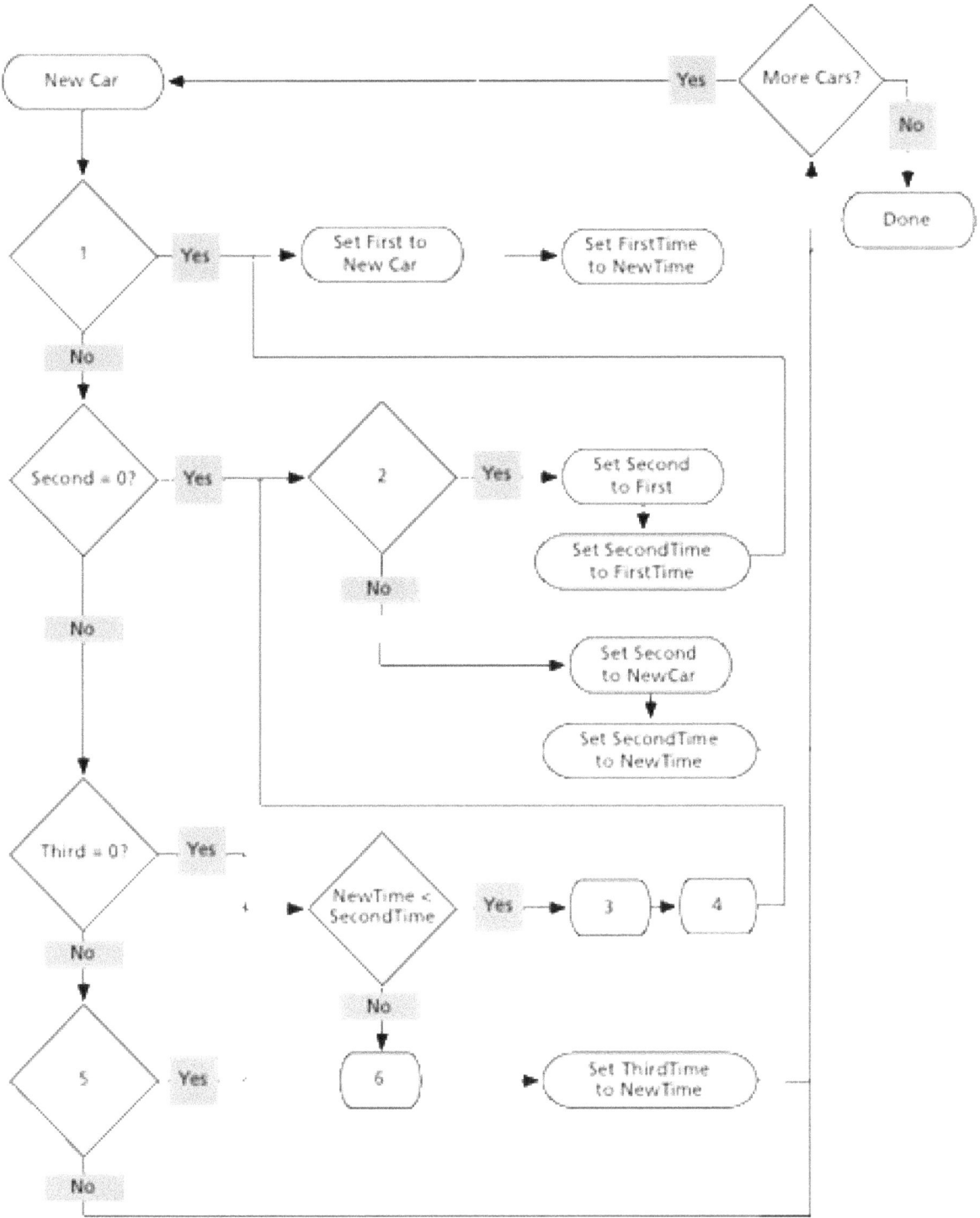

The figure to the right depicts the algorithm by which race cars are evaluated and winners tracked. In this case, the system is only interested in tracking which cars came in first, second and third, and their related times. Each time a new car posts a time, the system receives NewCar (the car number) and NewTime (the car's posted time). The system will maintain the First, Second and Third car numbers, and their related times in FirstTime, SecondTime and ThirdTime respectively. All variables are initially set to 0 and all car numbers are positive. Fill in the appropriate statement in each of the unfilled spaces.

1. What is the value of Cell 1?

A. If NewTime < FirstTime
B. If First = 0
C. If NewCar < First
D. If NewCar = 0

2. What is the value of Cell 2?

A. If NewTime > 0
B. If NewTime < SecondTime
C. If NewTime < FirstTime
D. If NewTime > FirstTime

3. What is the value of Cell 3?

A. Set Second to Third
B. Set Third to NewTime
C. Set Second to NewTime
D. Set Third to Second

4. What is the value of Cell 4?

A. Set ThirdTime to SecondTime
B. Set SecondTime to Thirdtime
C. Set SecondTime to NewTime
D. Set Thirdtime to NewTime

5. What is the value of Cell 5?

A. If NewTime > ThirdTime
B. If NewTime < ThirdTime
C. If NewCar > 0
D. If NewCar > Third

Diagram 2

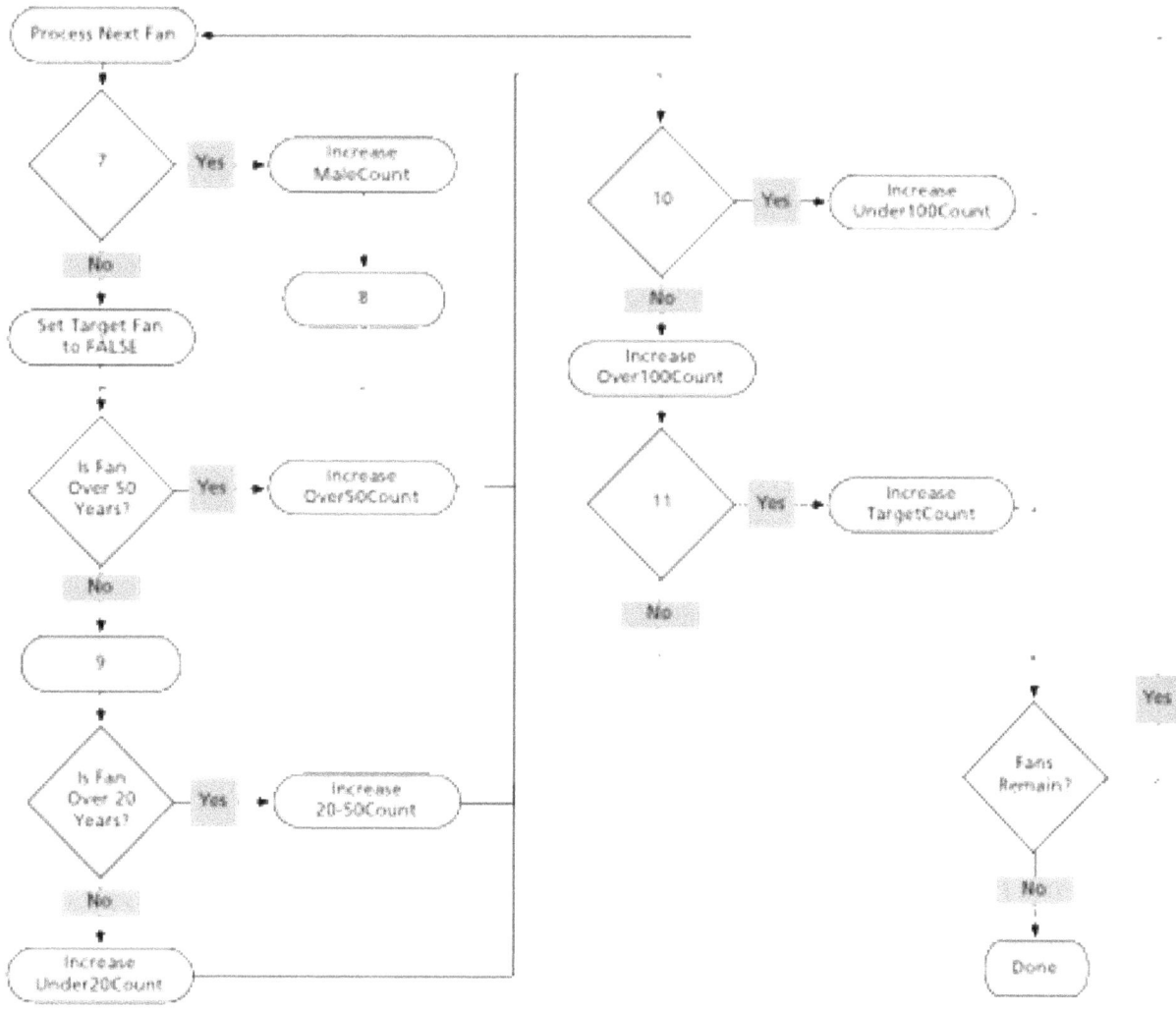

The figure to the right depicts the process by which demographic information is gathered as fans enter a sporting event. The goal is to count a number of statistics. First, count the number of Male fans (MaleCount). Then, classify each fan into one of three categories regarding his age (Over50Count, 20-50Count and Under20Count). Lastly, fans are classified by weight (Over100Count and Under100Count) depending on if their body weights are above or below 100 kilograms.

In addition to the data being collected above, the sponsor of the research also wants to know exactly how many Males over the age of 50 and weighing over 100 kilograms are in attendance, as this is their target market (TargetCount). So this must be tracked as each fan's information is processed.

All variables are initially set to 0. Fill in the appropriate statement in each of the unfilled cells.

1. What is the value of Cell 7?

A. Increase FanCount
B. Is MaleCount > 0?
C. Is the Fan a TargetFan?
D. Is the Fan Male?

2. What is the value of Cell 8?

A. Increase TargetCount
B. Set TargetFan to TRUE
C. Set MaleCount to 1
D. Set TargetFan to FALSE

3. What is the value of Cell 9?

A. Set TargetFan to FALSE
B. Increase Under50Count
C. Increase TargetCount
D. Set TargetFan to TRUE

4. What is the value of Cell 10?

A. Is the Fan over 100 kgs?
B. Is TargetFan = TRUE
C. Is the Fan under 100 kgs?
D. Is MaleCount > 1?

5. What is the value of Cell 11?

A. Is Over100Count > 0?
B. Is TargetFan = TRUE?
C. Is MaleCount >0 and Over50Count >0?
D. Is TargetCount > 0?

Chapter 6: IT Reasoning

IT Reasoning

IT Reasoning questions assess your ability to disassemble complex problems as well as apply logical principles in the organization of information. This is a crucial skill to show employers as working in any technical position requires the ability to break down complex scenarios and apply logical thinking in order to simplify and solve such scenarios efficiently.

IT Reasoning questions may appear in a variety of formats on the PAC Examination, including, but not limited to, data sufficiency questions, symbol questions and logical ordering. Each of these types of questions gives a slightly different perspective on your grasp of logic principles.

Again, these questions give you the opportunity to show employers that your potential is above and beyond your current skill set. You can use this section to show off your ability to adapt to new challenges and recognize which tools you need in order to do your work.

Data Sufficiency Questions

These questions evaluate your ability to appropriately determine what information is needed to solve a given problem. While the situations presented in these questions seem abstract, in every day working situations as a computer engineer, you will regularly need to sift through a vast amount of information and determine how to best use it to create a system in the most efficient manner. Sometimes there is not enough information, and you will have to obtain further facts in order to proceed with a solution; however, at other times there will be too much information and your task will be to choose the most appropriate information that best solves the problem.

In data sufficiency questions, you will be given a question along with 2 statements labeled with the letters A and B that contain information that relates to the question. You will be asked to determine to what degree, if any, statements A and B can be used to solve the question that is shown.

It is particularly important to know the instructions for this section before you enter the test as the format of these questions can be a little unnerving. Practicing will help you get comfortable with them.

The Official PAC Exam Guide

Logic Symbolizing Questions

Logic symbolizing questions test your understanding of the principles of logic by using conventional mathematical symbols to express problems, rather than numbers. When presented with challenges in developing systems, it is essential that you understand the logical relationships between the different parts of the system, in order to most effectively design a solution. These questions evaluate whether you are able to effectively and logically organize information that is presented to you.

Logic symbolizing questions will look very similar to math reasoning questions, only rather than finding a specific numeric value for the answer, you will be asked to define the equation needed to solve the problem presented to you using variables and operation symbols (ie, multiplication, division, addition or subtraction symbols).

Logic Ordering

When presented with information, it is important to understand what pieces of information are dependent on one another as well as the logical ordering of the question. This skill is what logic ordering questions evaluate. They determine if you can effectively create a logical sequence with information that is presented to you.

These questions will feature statements labeled with letters A, B and C that you must effectively order into a logical sequence. In addition, other versions of these types of questions may include a single statement for which you must choose from the answer options the statement that most logically results from the initial statement.

Quick Tips

1. Focus on the information presented within the question, rather than external information. Solving logic problems is about manipulating the information within the question in a rational manner, not bringing in outside knowledge.
2. For some problems, it helps to visually represent the different elements of the question with symbols on a separate piece of paper. Once you have visually represented the problem you should use logic and mathematical skills to solve the problem. Remember to rearrange the symbols in order to determine which relationship between the elements makes the most sense. A Venn diagram, for example, can be a very simple tool that will allow you to represent the information visually.
3. If you are presented with a question giving you answers about a topic unfamiliar to you, don't worry about it. Remember that these questions are ONLY about the information given to you in the question. So, for example, if the question tells you that all bats fly, and that all bats are rodents, don't worry if you didn't know that bats were rodents. Accept that the information given is true within the context of the question, and move on.

4. If you are presented with vocabulary you don't know, it is likely that you can get away with answering the question without knowing the vocabulary. Continuing with the above example: let's say that you don't know what a bat is. It doesn't really matter; all you have to know is that all X fly and all of X are rodents. Simply draw conclusions about X and see if the answer choices make sense within this context.

Sharpening Your Logic Skills

In the same way that you have to exercise to build up your physical muscles, you have to exercise your mind in order to make it stronger. The development of logic skills is a key arena in which you must regularly do this. There are numerous ways that you can strengthen your logic skills.

One of the best ways to do so is by consistently doing riddles, logic games or puzzles that stretch your capacity for developing logical conclusions based on a given set of information or principles. You can do these puzzles in any language, but doing them in English will probably increase your comfort while dealing with similar problems while taking the exam.

Take advantage of the Internet by visiting any of the sites that feature a variety of logic puzzles. With regular practice you'll be sure to impress employers with your ability to logically process and organize information.

Practice Questions

Instructions (these are the instructions you will see when taking the test):

This is the IT Reasoning section. It tests your ability to disassemble complex problems as well as apply logical principles in the organization of information. You will have 7 minutes to complete the 5 questions in this section.

Logical Relationships
In the following question three statements are given. Below that are options that denote that one of the statements is a conclusion based on the other three. Identify the option that gives the correct relationship.

1.

A) All cars are taxis
B) Some trucks are not taxis
C) Some cars are not trucks

    A. A can be concluded from B & C
    B. B can be concluded from A & C
    C. C can be concluded from A & B
    D. None of the above

2.
A) All elephants are immense
B) All elephants jump
C) All that is immense jumps

    A. A can be concluded from B & C
    B. B can be concluded from A & C
    C. C can be concluded from A & B
    D. None of the above

3.
A) Many kites are not eagles
B) Some eagles are falcons
C) Some kites are falcons

    A. A can be concluded from B & C
    B. B can be concluded from A & C
    C. C can be concluded from A & B
    D. None of the above

4.
A) Injecting is bad
B) Injecting is drugging
C) Drugging is bad

    A. A can be concluded from B & C
    B. B can be concluded from A & C
    C. C can be concluded from A & B
    D. None of the above

The question below consists of a main statement followed by five numbered statements. From the numbered statements, select the one that logically follows the main statement.

5. If the manager is in the office, then the workers will either code or document

A. The workers will either not code or not document; therefore, the manager is not in the office.
B. If the manager is not in the office, then the workers will not code and will not document.
C. The workers will not code and will not document; therefore, the manager is not in the office.
D. If the manager is not in the office, then the workers will either not document or not code.
E. None of the above.

The Official PAC Exam Guide

Data Sufficiency

This problem contains a question and two statements labeled A & B giving certain data. You have to select the correct answer from 1 to 4 depending on the sufficiency of the data given in the two statements to answer the question as follows:

6. A certain sum was divided among Alex, Bob and Cody. Who got the smallest share?

    A: Alex got 20% of the total amount
    B: Bob got 75% of the amount that Cody got

A. If the question can be answered by using one of the statements alone but cannot be answered by using the other statement alone.
B. If the question can be answered by using either statement alone.
C. If the question can be answered by using both statements together but cannot be answered by using either statement alone.
D. If the question cannot be answered even by using both the statements together.

7. What is the change in Xeno's score from test 1 to test 2?

    A: In the first test he scored 50%
    B: In the second test he scored 65 points

A. If the question can be answered by using one of the statements alone but cannot be answered by using the other statement alone.
B. If the question can be answered by using either statement alone.
C. If the question can be answered by using both statements together but cannot be answered by using either statement alone.
D. If the question cannot be answered even by using both the statements together.

8. A box of balls contains white and black balls in the proportion 1:3. How many white balls are to be added to reverse this proportion?

    A: The total number of balls in the box is 60
    B: The number of black balls in the box is 36

A. If the question can be answered by using one of the statements alone but cannot be answered by using the other statement alone.
B. If the question can be answered by using either statement alone.

C. If the question can be answered by using both statements together but cannot be answered by using either statement alone.
D. If the question cannot be answered even by using both the statements together.

9. Between two cities A & B, is the average speed of a train greater than 50 km/hr?

   A: Between noon and 4 pm it covers a distance of 200 km
   B: It takes 12 hours to cover 900 km between A and B

A. If the question can be answered by using one of the statements alone but cannot be answered by using the other statement alone.
B. If the question can be answered by using either statement alone.
C. If the question can be answered by using both statements together but cannot be answered by using either statement alone.
D. If the question cannot be answered even by using both the statements together.

The question below consists of a main statement followed by five numbered statements. From the numbered statements, select the one that logically follows the main statement.

10. Only if it rains, I will not go to work and I will watch TV.

A. It is not raining, therefore I will not go to work and I will watch TV.
B. I am not watching TV and I will go to work, therefore it does not rain.
C. It is not raining, therefore, I will go to work or I am not watching TV.
D. It rains and I am not watching TV, therefore I will go to work.
E. 2 & 3

Logic Symbolizing

11. Jane saves X% of her salary every month. When her salary goes up by 50% due to a promotion, she decides to increase her monthly expenditure by 25%. By how much does her monthly savings increase?

A. $1.5S - 1.25S(1 - X/100)$
B. $1.5S - 1.25S - SX/100$
C. $S(0.25 - X/100)$
D. $1.5S - 1.25S(1 - X)$

12. You decide to climb up 1000 steps to an ancient temple. There is one stop on the way after 500 steps. You walk up to the stop at a rate of x steps per minute, and then take a break for 10 minutes and then start climbing again but at a 20% slower speed. The number of minutes you take to complete the climb is:

A. 10 + 500/(x +0.8/x)
B. 10 + 500/x + (500*0.8)/x
C. 10 + 500/x + 500/(x*0.2)
D. 10 + 500/x + 500/(x*0.8)

13. A caravan has 200 adult males, 250 adult females and 150 children. Each adult male eats x kg of food per day. An adult female eats 20% less food per day than an adult male, and a child eats 50% less food per day than an adult male. At the start of a particular journey estimated to take 50 days, the caravan had enough food to last 60 days. After 20 days of traveling the caravan took in an additional 100 adult males, 100 adult females and 100 children. If everybody decreases his or her daily consumption by 10% from the initial amount, how much more food needs to be loaded for the caravan to have sufficient food for the rest of the journey for the expanded group?

A. (100X+ 100(0.8X)+100(0.5X))*40*0.9
B. (300X+ 350(0.8X)+250(0.5X))*40*0.9
C. (300X+ 350(0.8X)+250(0.5X))*40*0.9 - (200X+ 250(0.8X)+150(0.5X))*40
D. (300X+ 350(0.8X)+250(0.5X))*30*0.9 - (200X+ 250(0.8X)+150(0.5X))*40

14. A shopkeeper marks up the price of an article over his cost price CP by 150%. He then offers a discount of D% on it. When the article is still unsold, he offers a second discount of 20% on it. Finally he has to offer a third discount of X% and then the item is sold at a profit of P. P is represented by:

A. CP*1.5(1-D)(0.8)(1-X) – CP
B. CP*2.5(1-D)(0.8)(1-X) – CP
C. CP*1.5(1-D/100)(0.8)(1-X/100) – CP
D. CP*2.5(1-D/100)(0.8)(1-X/100) – CP

15. There are two bags, the first containing R red marbles and the second containing B blue marbles. From the first bag X marbles are randomly selected and transferred to the second bag, and then from the second bag, Y marbles are randomly selected and transferred to the first bag. After this, the likely number of red marbles in the first bag is:

A. R-X+Y
B. R-X+X/(B+X)
C. R-X+XY(B+X)
D. R-X+XY/(B+X)

Logical Ordering
Select the alternative that logically follows from the two given statements, but not from one statement alone.

16.
All humans are people.
Some people are public.

1. Some humans are public
2. No human is public
3. All humans are public
4. None of the above

17.
All bits are bytes
No bytes are data

A. All bits are data
B. Some bits are data
C. No bit is data
D. None of the above

18.
Some thieves are crooks
Some crooks are not robbers

A. Some crooks are robbers
B. Some thieves are not robbers
C. Both 1 and 2
D. None of the above

19.
Some apples are berries
All berries are cherries

    A.   No apple is a cherry
    B.   Some apples are cherries
    C.   All apples are cherries
    D.   None of the above

20.
Some timber are logs
All logs are made of wood

    A.   Some timber is made of wood
    B.   Some timber is not made of wood
    C.   No timber is made of wood
    D.   None of the above

Chapter 7: Attention to detail

Attention to Detail

Attention to Detail questions test your ability to notice key details in a large amount of information. Not only is it important to grasp the concept of a system, but it is also vitally important to pay attention to the details when implementing a process. It is those small, but crucial details that define the quality and effectiveness of systems. In addition, these questions test how well you can identify a pattern and recognize when there is an element that falls outside of it.

You will be presented with a chart, table or diagram with a list of information that will be used to answer each of the questions in the section. There will be a series of questions in which you will be asked to determine if a given item from the presented table is accurately presented.

Quick Tips for Attention to Detail

1. When answering Attention to Detail questions, try using a sheet of paper to cover the multiple lines of the table on the screen and just focus on one line at a time. This will break up the image on the screen and allow you to better identify any of the potential errors in the table. This is particularly useful as you will be viewing these questions on a computer screen, and it will be considerably more difficult. Additionally, it will allow you to focus on one line of the table at a time.

2. Don't worry if you don't know some of the words presented in the table. Knowing exactly what each item is or does is irrelevant in answering these questions.

Developing an Eye for Detail

While some people have a natural propensity for noticing details, it is possible to develop a stronger eye for detail through your everyday activities. After completing projects, homework or tests, go back through your work in order to catch misspelled words, punctuation errors or other flaws. Paying attention to details is all about improving the quality of your work, and in working as a computer engineer, improving the systems you're developing. So while it might seem tedious, developing a strong eye for detail will ultimately strengthen your ability to design and implement processes that are logical, efficient and effective.

Again, this is a good opportunity to show an employer that you work with care and consideration. It is not important that you know the functions or even the correct pronunciation of the items being given on the tables; what is important is that you can effectively observe inconsistencies in their cataloguing.

Practice Questions

Instructions (these are the instructions you will see when taking the test)::

This is the Attention to Detail section. It is designed to test your ability to adhere to detail within a large volume of information. You will be presented with one table of information along with ten individual lines of information on one page. You will need to identify if the individual lines of information are correct or not. You will have 2 minutes to complete this section.

Below is an image of what the Attention to Detail questions will look like on the computer screen. Just like the Reading Comprehension and Logic Diagramming questions, during the exam you will need to scroll down in order to view the question and answer options.

Online Assessment
Baseline Fundamentals

36. Use the table to answer the question below.

Part Number	Part Name
120-AA5528-109/A	Rotary Cup – Aluminum Grade
150-BG3310-116/A	1.2cm Brass Thread Screws Reversed Coil
108-2271905-6688/LL	Magnetic Philips Screw Sized 1.2
228-CH19527-862/LL	Claw Hammer, Yellow Handle
228-CH19577-862/LL	Claw Hammer, Blue Handle
228-CH19337-928/CM	12 Piece Philips Screw Driver Set
228-CH19355-988/SD	12 Piece Flat Screw Driver Set
150-BG3309-155/LJ	1.5cm Brass Thread Screws Forward Coil
527-SMO522828-622/GK	Long Tooth Saw Professional Grade
150-BG3301-116/A	1.2cm Brass Thread Screws Forward Coil
108-228427884-526/GG	Electric hammer with Accessory Kit
228-CH19557-862/LL	Claw Hammer, Red Handle
228-CH19537-862/LL	Claw Hammer, Green Handle
108-2279105-6688/LL	Magnetic Philips Screw Driver Sized 1.2
108-2214278-155/BG	Power Tool Base Station Charger
229-CIH55628-105/SC	Electric Circuit Board with Jumpers

The correct part number for the Part "1.2cm Brass Thread Screws Forward Coil" is:

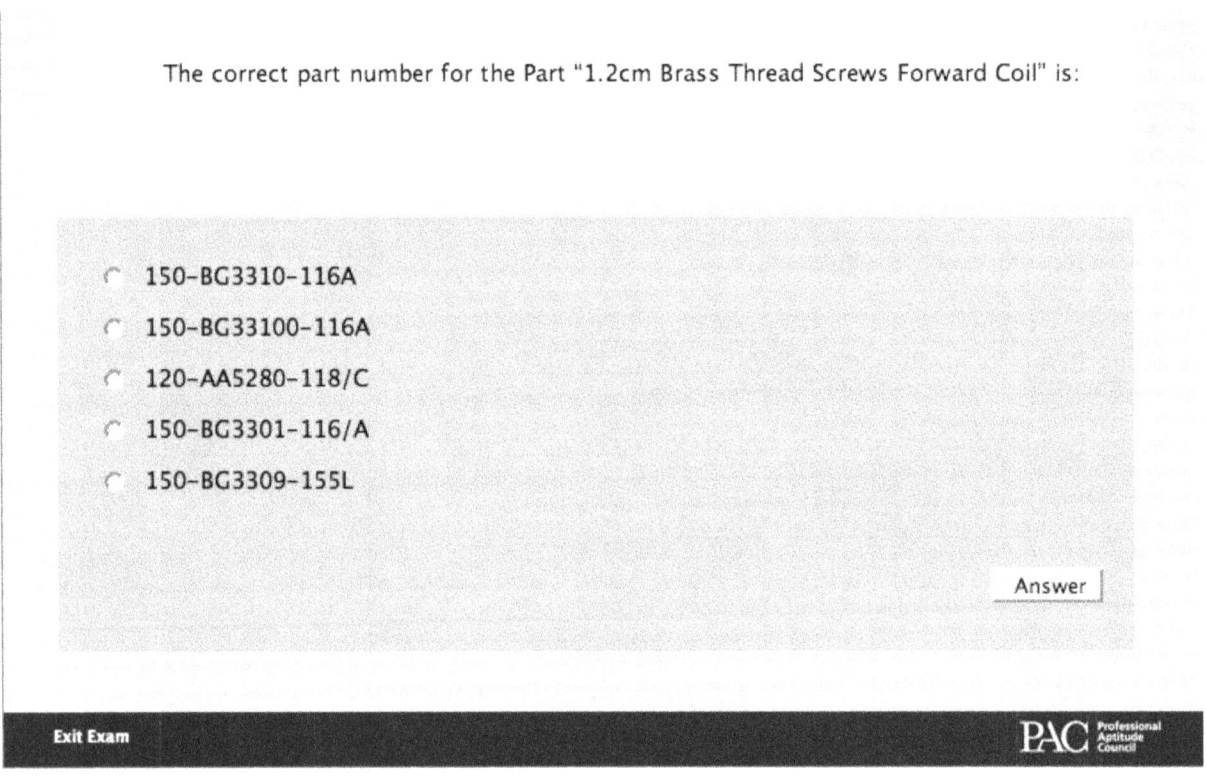

Part Name	Part Code
Spreader Finger Cam No. 4	2200-BB6394-107-H
Spreader Finger Cam Set Screw	2222-DD6266-109-G
Spreader Finger Cam Roll	2244-BB3016-107-I
Feed Arm Lever Cam No. 7	2266-AA3390-107-G
Feed Arm Lever Cam Roll	2244-BB4588-112-H
Slide Cam Roll	2222-AA1801-116-J
Spotter Bar-Complete	2200-CC6000-105-H
Spotter Head Clamp	2244-CC8022-100-G
Spotter Bracket	2266-AA6634-116-H
Spotter Bracket Screw Plate	2200-CC1608-111-H
Spotter Plates	2266-BB8089-115-I
Spotter Plate Screws-Flat Head	2244-BB6599-108-J
Spotter Plungers 9-16 Inches	2266-BB8381-100-J
Spotter Plunger Springs	2266-AA3349-105-G
Spotter Thumb Screws	2222-CC3524-108-H

1. The correct part code for the part 'Spotter Plate Screws-Flat Head' is

A. 2244-BB3016-107-I
B. 2244-BB4588-112-H
C. 2244-CC8022-100-G
D. 2244-BB6599-108-J

2. The correct part code for the part 'Feed Arm Lever Cam No. 7' is
A. 2266-AA6634-116-H
B. 2266-BB8381-100-J
C. 2266-AA3390-107-G
D. 2266-AA3349-105-G

3. The correct part code for the part 'Feed Arm Lever Cam Roll' is
A. 2244-BB3016-107-I
B. 2244-BB4588-112-H
C. 2244-CC8022-100-G
D. 2244-BB6599-108-J

4. The correct part code for the part 'Spotter Plunger Springs' is
A. 2266-BB8089-115-I
B. 2266-BB8381-100-J
C. 2266-AA3349-105-G
D. 2266-AA6634-116-H

5. The correct part code for the part 'Spreader Finger Cam Set Screw' is
A. 2222-DD6266-109-G
B. 2222-AA1801-116-J
C. 2244-CC8022-100-G
D. 2222-CC3524-108-H

6. The correct part code for the part 'Spotter Head Clamp' is
A. 2244-CC3016-107-I
B. 2244-CC4588-112-H
C. 2244-CC6599-108-J
D. 2244-CC8022-100-G

7. Which of the following is not a valid part code?
A. 2200-BB6394-107-H
B. 2244-BB4688-112-H
C. 2266-BB8089-115-I
D. 2222-CC3524-108-H

8. Which of the following is not a valid part code?
A. 2222-DD6266-109-G
B. 2244-CC8022-100-G
C. 2266-BB8381-101-J

D. 2266-AA3349-105-G

9. Which of the following is not a valid part code?
A. 2244-BB3016-107-I
B. 2266-AA6634-116-H
C. 2200-CC1508-111-H
D. 2244-BB6599-108-J

10. Which of the following is not a valid part code?
A. 2266-AA3390-107-G
B. 2222-AA1801-116-J
C. 2200-CC6000-105-H
D. 2200-CC6100-105-H

Answer Key

Reading Comprehension

1. D
2. A
3. D
4. B
5. C
6. A
7. B
8. D
9. D
10. D

Math Reasoning

1. B
2. B
3. C
4. D
5. C
6. D
7. C
8. B
9. C
10. B
11. C
12. C
13. B
14. D
15. C
16. D
17. A
18. C
19. D
20. D

Sentence Structure

1. A
2. C
3. C
4. B
5. A
6. D

7. D
8. B
9. A
10. A
11. B
12. B
13. C
14. A
15. D
16. A
17. D
18. B
19. D
20. C

Logic Diagramming
Diagram 1

1. B
2. C
3. D
4. A
5. B

Diagram 2
1. D
2. B
3. A
4. C
5. B

IT Reasoning

1. D
2. B
3. D

4. C
5. C
6. C
7. D
8. B
9. A
10. E
11. A
12. B

13. D
14. D
15. D
16. D
17. C
18. A
19. B
20. A

Attention to Detail (ATD)

1. D
2. C
3. B
4. C
5. A
6. D
7. B
8. C
9. C
10. D

Additional Resources

Bright Sparks 2008

Since 2003, PAC and Bright Sparks have helped tens of thousands of Indian students get the best jobs at leading global companies. With online resources such as practice assessments and interview preparation guides, Bright Sparks is designed to help you excel completely free of charge. Register today at www.pacsparks.com.

Professional Aptitude Council (PAC)

Gain access to career resources and view your PAC Examination score at the official site of the Professional Aptitude Council (PAC). Get started at www.pacexam.com today.

www.ingramcontent.com/pod-product-compliance
Lightning Source LLC
Chambersburg PA
CBHW080554170426
43195CB00016B/2787